The Adventures of Bear

Farabee Publishing Chandler, AZ 85224
www.Farabeepublishing.com

ISBN: 979-8-89238-032-4

Printed in the United States of America

Book Cover designed by: Brennan McLaughlin

My name is Tatum. This is the true story of the adventures
of Bear, my pet hamster. Well, most of it..

Bear was born and started his life away from his family at the pet store.

I went to the pet store one day and chose Bear out of all of the hamsters in the store.

I took him to his forever home.

The very night he came to his new home, he searched for a way to get out and explore the wonders of the new world.

Bear escapes!! Finding his new home through a crack in the wall where he sets up his new place to live.

One day, on his journey out into the world, Bear becomes
thirsty. He is in desperate need of water. Out of nowhere is
a giant bowl of water, the most water he has ever seen!

As he approaches the great big bowl, he decides to dive in
headfirst in hopes for a sip of water.

He realizes that it is too deep!! He can't get out and starts to kick with all of his might!! Waving his arms, squeaking for help!!

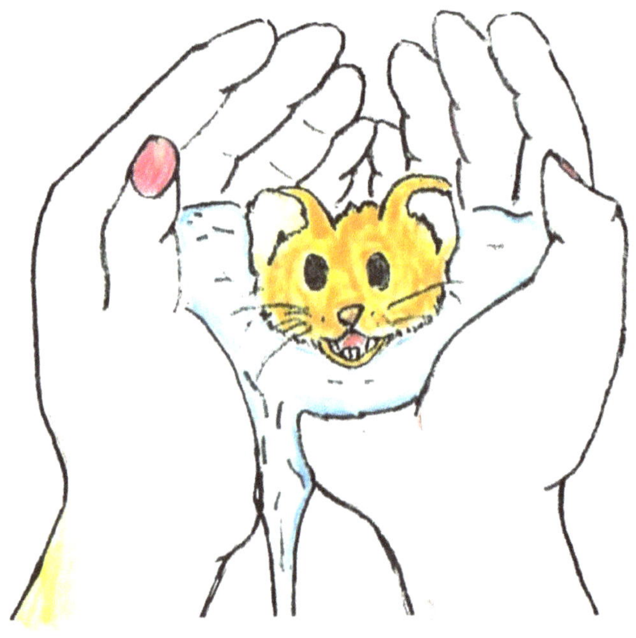

From above came a large being on two legs, but it didn't look like him at all. This being was my mom, she is not a hamster. She reaches down and pulls him out to save his life!

Even though he was saved and safe, Bear still wanted to venture into the big world and see what was out there. I thought Bear was gone forever.

As he was roaming at night, Bear was approached by a big furry fellow named Scout. Scout is a dog and quickly becomes good friends and attempts to teach Bear about the new world.

Scout decides to help him with getting food and how to
safely get water. Sometimes leaving his dog food out for
Bear to take home.

Bear would spend the next two years exploring the wonders of the new world like no other hamster had done before.

As Bear crawls through the passages underneath the house, his first encounter is a Field Mouse!! They both were very scared at first. But Bear was much bigger than the Field Mouse. As they cower towards each other, sensing fear, they both sat on the ground. They communicated as best they could and found that they were better off friends than enemies.

Soon, they would travel together, learning from each other and finding that working together made the travels much more fun!

As Bear gets older and tired from his exploring, he wants to come back home, to be with me and the place where he started.

One day, with the crack that he found his new home
through now gone, he decides to chew a hole in the wall to
find his way home.

As he was digging through the wall, all of these years later, the last thing I expect to see was a furry little face of my Bear poking out!

I quickly pulled him out and gave him a big hug. I thought I would never see him again!

I fixed up his glass home and made it nice and comfortable. I look after him every day to make sure he is happy, and he is.

In his relatively short life span, Bear was able to do a lot. He traveled. He faced situations that he didn't think he would be able to make it through. He learned the kindness of those that did not look like him. He learned that not everything different is scary, and that with the help of his new friends,

EVERYTHING IS POSSIBLE

Bear And Friends Coloring Book

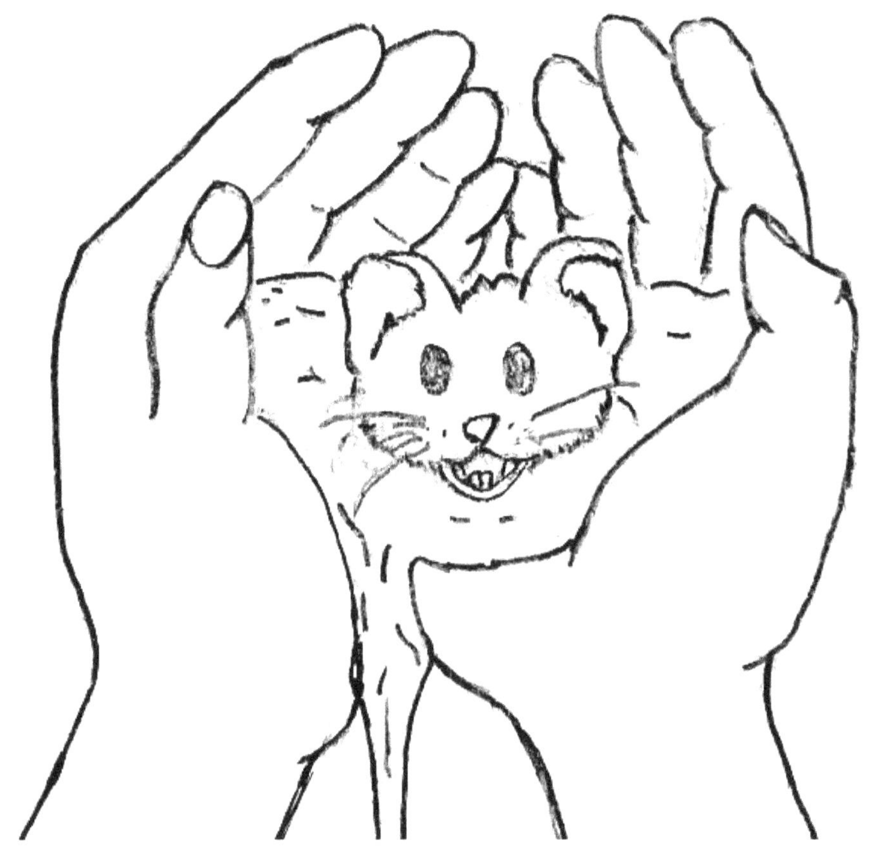